Divine Whispers

Poems of Love and Spirit

By Dr. Bill Clark

Beyond Limits Press

Divine Whispers: Poems of Love and Spirit

Written by Dr. Bill Clark

Published in the United States by

Beyond Limits Press

Clearwater, Florida

ISBN: 979-8-9990552-1-7

First Edition – 2025

To connect with the author, visit:

www.drbillclark.life

Table of Contents

Dedication

For the seekers,

the lovers,

and the dreamers who listen for the whispers.

Forward

The infinite presence of God, Spirit, or Higher Power lives, moves, and has Its being within all things. It is omniscient, omnipotent, and omnipresent — the glorious unfolding of the force that creates everything we see, touch, feel, and love.

It moves us to a space of awe and wonder to behold... and through this, we come to experience true Love.

During the course of my own spiritual evolution, I have come to know this presence intimately — for I am Its Divine expression and conduit, that It may know It exists through me.

The poems in this collection were written between 2009 and 2024, spanning years of deep inquiry, surrender, awakening, and healing. They emerged as sacred whispers during moments of heartbreak, love, silence, joy, and revelation — all part of my journey into spiritual union with the Divine.

This work is both personal and universal. It is my deepest desire for you to feel what Spirit has inspired through me and as me. For at that moment... you will be touched by the beauty of Grace and Love.

A Note to the Reader:

Some poems in this collection explore the sacred nature of sensuality and romantic intimacy. These pieces are marked with an "(E)" to honor your awareness, and to uphold the intention behind every word: reverence, beauty, and the full expression of Divine Love in human form.

With deepest love, gratitude, and blessings,
Dr. Bill

Poems of Love

The minute I heard my first love story,
I started looking for you,
not knowing how blind that was.
Lovers don't finally meet somewhere.
They're in each other all along.

— Rumi, from The Essential Rumi

Radiant Light of Love

The light and beauty of love shines brightly

from the deepest parts of your soul

It is infinite in its Divine nature.

And though I may see thousands of gorgeous sunsets

none would touch my heart more

than the radiant light of love

I see within your sparkling eyes

and glowing upon your face.

Angel in My Dreams

The sound of her voice
Lifts the desert air
Whispers of love
So soft and fair

Is that an Angel
Who calls my name?
Or just a sweet girl
They are one and the same

My Spirit cried out
Wanting to be free
So many months wondering
Oh, where can she be?

Her love is unconditional
It fills my very soul
Remembering we were truly one
Longing to be made whole

The long journey now over

Our glorious union blessed

Divinely connected and guided

I am now at peaceful rest

For my heart is bursting

With wondrous love and sunbeams

She is with me now

In my Spirit…..and in my dreams

Divine Fusion

She reaches into my Soul
With a connection undefined
Knows my every thought
With a love quite divine

My heart inspired to soar
Her Spirit moving with grace
Lifting me to higher consciousness
I AM infinite space

Time does not exist
As fluid as the ocean
Embarked on this journey
Without care or a notion

Her beauty radiates light
A beacon for my heart
Drawn into her fiery essence
Fused as One to never part

Our sacred union truly blessed

Wondrous in its measure

Healing love shifting All

With pearls of joy to treasure

For this precious Angel

A love blissfully released

Transforms me completely

With joyous grace and peace

Forever Entwined (E)

Her sweet smile so wondrous to behold
Those sparkling eyes Oh how I adore
A precious Angel calls softly my sweetheart
Taking her in my arms gentle sighs implore

Embracing my love with grateful heart
Feeling her glorious body next to mine
Sweeping her hair back reveals such beauty
The taste of succulent lips so divine

Gentle kisses along her graceful neck
Arms wrapped around my love from behind
She guides my hands to caress her naked body
Oh so soft, so warm, and sweetly sublime

Feeling my beautiful lover beneath me
Her fingers trace the curves of my arms
My hardness engulfed in her erotic dream
Passionately lost in sensual charm

Deeper through the sweet journey of ecstasy

Luscious scents of her permeate the air

My lover cries with incredible bliss

For no other love could ever compare

Entwined in the warmth of each other's arms

Our connection a perfect spiritual sun

 Knowing the presence of love so divine

Joined together…forever more as one

Rumba of Love

Moving on the dance floor with grace
A mystery starts to unfold
Rumba motion ignites passion
Visions of love soon to be told

Pouring rain washes over love's embrace
Palm leaves sheltering passion's kiss
Cool with warmth in firm steamy touch
Hearts soaring with fiery bliss

Brilliant mystical sunset
Love light glowing upon your face
Touching the soft depths of my heart
Your sparkling eyes brighten this place

Blue green water lies before us
Dolphin magic brings us sweet love
Balmy breezes caress our skin
Tender Spirit flows from above

As the full moon sets over the palm

 My beloved sleeps below me

Joyful sighs rise on Angel's wings

Feeling wondrous love within thee

These moments of infinite love

Truly guided by loving hands

Blessings for an eternity

Spiritual union forever stands

When You Smile

When you smile
It warms my grateful heart
When you smile
I don't want to part

When you smile
Your presence is glamorous
When you smile
I can't help but be amorous

When you smile
The ocean depths ring
When you smile
The heavens above sing

When you smile
Nature's beauty gives way
When you smile
You become the light of my day

When you smile

The infinite shines through

When you smile

Remember sweet girl I See You

When you smile

You keep me longing for more

When you smile

You're the woman I absolutely adore!

I See You

I See into those sparkling eyes
The paradise of your soul
My wondrous gaze is rarefied
You're the one who makes me whole

I See that beautiful smile
It warms this tender heart
Filling me full of life
Knowing we will never part

I See a divine goddess
For which no other beauty compares
I am lost in the ether of your presence
Moving with grace, you are unaware

I See a loving heart
Feeling it beat for all
It touches mine in so many ways
I cannot count them all

I See a voice with kind words

An angel sent from above

Their harmony is music to my ears

You, a glimmering light of true love

I See an amazing woman

Whose passion fires me anew

You're vibrant energy consumes me

My sweet girl….I See You

Divine Union (E)

Great Spirit is in the house
Breathing the cool night air
Feeling your soft presence next to mine
Knowing you'll always be there

The stars radiate light in your eyes
Whispers of love in my ear
Our hearts become intertwined
Knowing there is nothing to fear

The night heats up with passion
Your luscious lips embraced in mine
Deeply our souls are fashioned
Knowing this true love is divine

Our hearts begin to beat as one
Your supple breasts find their caress
Sweet scents of my glorious angel
Knowing that I am truly blessed

Our hot breath is whisked away
Passionate cries of joy and bliss
Magical moments of pure ecstasy
Knowing that nothing is amiss

The dew of love glows in your face
The smiles of beautiful release
Our hearts forever joined in love
Knowing we are in infinite peace

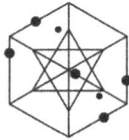

Dreamland Voyage

Off to dreamland we go my love
Within these arms holding you tight
Sweet kisses warming our tender hearts
Forever joined in peaceful flight

I see the canvas of our dream
Waiting for this love to create
Painted joy in vivid color
Unlimited it permeates

Such glowing angelic beauty
Radiating from your sweet face
Explodes into my awareness
Love fills my heart in every space

Gentle caresses from soft hands
Entwined in everlasting love
A beautiful song without words
Floating through lush clouds high above

Higher and higher we travel
Until we reach a distant star
Spirit moon guides our love journey
Illumined sun warms from afar

Divine grace our sufficiency
Joyous ecstasy...so rare
Together forever as One
Love manifest beyond compare

Fields of Gold and Grace

She calls my name in the early light
Waking me from my dream of love
Her soft, sweet voice fills my heart
An Angel truly sent from above

Dancing through endless fields of gold
The gentle rain caressing love's embrace
Feeling the energy of her presence
We move together through time and space

Looking into my lover's eyes
We meet in that wondrous place within
Deeply kissing sweet, strawberry lips
Passion's fire steams the water on our skin

Feeling this magical moment
Our bodies firmly wrapped as one
Angel's light sparkles all around us
Illumined love as bright as the sun

Laying in the tall sweeping grass
Mother Earth a cradle of love
Exploding points of ecstasy
Adds to the brilliant stars above

Alignment with beauty and grace
Its energy is beyond measure
This is the essence of true love
To be One with all the treasure

Infinite Embrace (E)

My sweet girl lies before me
Her nakedness divinely curved
Lost in her presence
I am completely unnerved

When I look into her eyes
I am drowning within
Her love unspoken
Claims my heart to begin

Lush lips meet with fire
Our passionate breath entwined
Kissing her graceful neck
It is absolutely divine

The suppleness of her skin
So soft without care
Tracing her lines with my lips
No other compares

Sweet scents of this woman
Her fragrance fills the air
My tongue buried in wetness
It's more than I can bear

Lifting her onto my manhood
Finding her treasure deep within
Wrapped around each other tightly
Moaning cries of love begin

Experiencing every part of my angel
Our souls joined as one
Infinite points of ecstasy
A beautiful mystery undone

Falling into complete bliss
My sweet girl lying in my arms
Our gaze of Love unconditional
Her beautiful smile radiates charm

Dream Dance

She sits frozen, lost in dream
A sleeping beauty so fair
Gently touching her shoulder
She comes alive with graceful air

Dancing with this divine goddess
Smiles radiating sweet charm
Our bodies fluid as one
Lost in each other's arms

Her fiery eyes full of passion
A glowing spirit within
Show me a familiar place
Opening my heart again

Stars shining bright above us
Illumine this dance of love
Our hearts soaring with the wind
Guided by that Grace above

Laughter and joy resonate

With sweet love and abandon

Angel's message comes alive

Each finding our lost companion

With a gentle tenderness

Moving into love's embrace

This dream dance sealed with a kiss

The peace of infinite space

My Everything

You're the one that captures my heart
Knowing our love will never part
You're the sun shining on a summer's day
Warming my soul in so many ways

Your smile moves me to glorious joy
Especially when you're just being coy
Your radiant eyes begin to lure me in
Longing for angelic lovemaking to begin

Your supple lips taste quite divine
Like the sweetness of the finest wine
Your body moves with amazing grace
Taking me to a beautiful place

Your wonderful voice rings through my ears
Calling me "sweetheart" giving chills like you're near
Your fun laughter puts a smile on my face
Like bursting points of light from infinite space

Your vulnerability delivers sweet tears

Allowing me to wipe away all your fears

Your passionate excitement builds vibrant energy

And gives me complete comfort in our amazing synergy

For you are all these things and so much more

Lifting me up where I can't touch the floor

Feeling as if I could reach the sky

You are My Everything….and so I can fly!

Elemental Love

Love is elemental. Like water.

Let love wash over and flow through you.

Hold love in your hands gently.

Drink in its wondrous beauty.

Love is elemental. Like fire.

Let love fuel the passion in your heart.

Feel the energy lift your Spirit.

Bask in its warmth.

Love is elemental. Like wind.

Let love lift you into higher consciousness.

Soar into ecstatic realms.

Embrace its true essence.

Love is elemental. Like earth.

Let love ground you in rock sensuality.

Birth the pleasures in your Soul.

Embody its ferocious power.

Love is elemental. Like magic.

Let love guide you on your journey.

Follow your inner compass.

Dare to believe in yourself.

Love is elemental. Like energy.

Let love attract the vibrational match of your desires.

Feel the creation of a new world.

Manifest the greatness within You.

Love is elemental. Like spirit.

Let love release innate joy and bliss

from the depths of your Being.

Transform the experience of your life.

Journey to Love

For so many long years I wondered
Oh where this true love of mine could be
I searched for what seemed like forever
Until the day God brought you to me

An Angel of love who came that night
Waking me up from my peaceful sleep
Touching my heart in such unique ways
Tears of joy knew you were mine to keep

Once again on windy desert air
Your sublime presence found my kind heart
Energy and grace so powerful
I See You claims we will never part

Several more years passed without you
A beautiful mystery unsolved
Aching for your physical presence
Love's final measure had to evolve

Then one day a miracle occurred
Introduction from a distance
Long communications then ensued
Confirming our true love's existence

Warm blessings for our divine union
Connections beautifully revealed
Finally this sweet girl in my arms
Our longing hearts completely unsealed

Embodied in love forever more
We begin this shared journey of life
Reaching the horizons of new shores
So I wonder would you be my wife?

Poems of Spirit

There was something formless and perfect
before the universe was born.
It is serene. Empty.
Solitary. Unchanging.
Infinite. Eternally present.
It is the mother of the universe.
For lack of a better name, I call it the Tao.

— *Lao Tzu, Tao Te Ching*

The Mystic's Path

To love and not be loved,

such is the journey of the mystic.

To see what others do not see.

To know what they do not understand.

Though a million stars may fall,

the light shines for no one;

While their path to freedom is hidden.

A wise man knows the Way.

Autumn's Revelation

Yellow color of the Fall bloom
Mysteries of Summer revealed
Morning fog blankets barren trees
What is seen is once more concealed

Roosters call out the morning sun
Hummingbirds enjoy dance and play
Buddha smiles upon the still pond
The dawn of a spiritual day

Red dragonflies zip to and fro
Lotus flower opens to sun
Insects on the quest for water
All in alignment with the One

The Art of Letting Go

Letting go of drama

Letting go of expectations

Letting go of control

And all unsettling sensations

Letting go of what no longer serves

Letting go of fear

Letting go of frustration

Knowing that Spirit's presence is near

Letting go of judgments

Letting go of stories

Letting go of guilt

There really are no worries

Letting go of false beliefs

Letting go of sin

Letting go of lost love

Finding that still small voice within

Forgiving all the past
Filling our hearts with love
Forgiving ourselves most of all
Trusting in the process above

Taking a path with heart
Movement fluid with Grace
Knowing we are never alone
Embracing this peaceful space

For we are this Divine presence
Not this illusion we see
That seeks only our Good in this life
And remembers…to just Be

The Mystic's Acceptance

When life's challenges deal you a horrible blow
When the cracks in your armor start to show
Let it be and know It is

When those who once loved you begin to fade
When the power of the infinite brings light to your shade
Let it be and know It is

When you feel that your heart can take no more
When you see a wave crashing on a distant shore
Let it be and know It is

When some days you feel like you want to die
When you see a hawk circling way up in the sky
Let it be and know It is

For these are the callings of the mystic

The journeys of your soul with the infinite

For you are not what you see

But only the answer on how to be

So let go and embrace the light

For it is eternal power and full of might

This is your time to move forward with activation

And become one with the glorious path of co-creation

Let it be and know It is

From Night to Light

The still and quiet of the night
Washes over my troubled soul
My heart broken with so much grief
No longer feeling whole

All beliefs shattered and torn
Spirit crushed under dark dread
Not knowing how to go on
My faith hanging by a thread

Love's vibration silenced flat
Heart cries with lamentations
Embracing the darkest night
Reveals all expectations

Night shifts into lighted day
Glimmers of hope renew life
The sea breeze blows on my face
God's breath releasing all strife

Feeling this presence lift me
The inner voice grows within
God's heart fulfills sacred life
Love compelling to begin

Cracks in my heart heal once more
Removing me from the fray
Waves reflecting Spirit's light
Illuminate brightest day

Dreamland's Call

The melodic chirp of crickets sound
Sister moon my heavenly guide
For off to dreamland I am bound
Where no earthly presence will confide

Sleep fills these dreary eyes
Deep breathing renews my soul
Spirit lifts me up on high
To a place where I am whole

The call of Father Owl expands my mind
Filling it with great wisdom
There it is matched in like kind
With all the glory of the kingdom

Messages from Great Spirit I've received
Brother Hawk's work finally complete
For Its expansiveness I could not conceive
My heart slowly pounds the beat

The cool night air gently caresses my face

Soft fluttering of angel's wings

Reaching out from dimensional space

My heart humbly rejoices and sings

Mother Earth engulfs me in her arms

The heavens a blanket above me

A billion points of light sparkle with charm

The presence of the infinite weighs upon thee

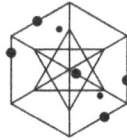

Divine Sacrifice

Embracing the deep dark unknown
In that one moment called to serve
Giving others freedom to live
While remaining calm and unnerved

Sacrifices too numerous
Throughout history we have seen
We must never ever forget
And be grateful for what they mean

Divine golden light guides the way
God's all-knowing presence in how
Peace passes all understanding
That perfect life is one life now

October Awakening

A gloomy October morning
Drowning in deep despair
God's tears drench my humble abode
All alone...feeling no one cares

Thinking of loved ones lost
My heart aches with tremendous grief
Wondering where I went wrong
What are these faulty beliefs?

I have reached the breaking point
My heaving chest torn apart
The essence of who I am
Lost...in all conscious thought

I move through space and time
Numbness deadens all my nerves
A glimmer of Truth for who I AM
Fully letting go...of what no longer serves

For it was in this moment
My consciousness and world began to shift
From the crucible of the alchemist's fire
A glorious phoenix began to lift!

Knowing Spirit moves through me and as me
By God's grace I am made whole
This Presence fills my true being
Faith…renews my very Soul

For we are not who we claim we are
Or the scars from our distant past
Or the definition from those afar
These are only memories…and do not last

We are that Divine Presence of God!
It is eternally who we were meant to be
Know this for you my friends
For I now know it…of me

The Seed's Awakening

A promise of divine thought
Moments waiting to collide
Sleeping in Angel's embrace
A seed dreaming from inside

Warming touch of Mother Earth
Surrounds with loving nature
Giving life to waking dreams
Miracles of sweet stature

Flowing water of the Tao
Fills all the empty spaces
Leaving nothing to question
Only God's endless faces

The light of glorious day
Breaches heaven's golden womb
Nourishing all known desires
The path visible now blooms

Air of magnificent grace
The answer to all the why
Sweeping energy of One
Form lifts up to Father Sky

Wondrous dreams in completion
Flowering with expression
Open to a brave new world
The seed's manifestation

Nature's Symphony

Gentle rain falls upon the roof
Waking me from my wondrous sleep
Mockingbird sings his morning song
Beauty and joy are mine to keep

 White egret shakes off thunderous wind
As lightning bolts dance in the sky
Feeling this static energy
I AM present and I know why

The palm leaves rustle with the wind
Sister moon shining her sweet face
Breathing deeply morning salt air
Takes me to this infinite space

Cicadas make their evening sound
Magical with such sweet treasure
Warm summer night caresses my skin
Love within beyond all measure

A citrus moon kisses the night sky

The stars a billion points of light

Seeing Source with wonder and awe

Wisdom and truth flow through with might

A lavender sunset ending

Bringing a close to nature's song

Pelicans dive the dark waters

Being One with the Tao…I AM strong

Awakening in the Rain

Feel the rain in all its wonder.

The energetic connection to the spirit of nature.

A constant unfolding of spirit and consciousness.

Where divine beauty reveals itself.

And while it gives life in transparent motion.

Only the awakened see its true form.

Spiritual Sun Awakening

Spiritual sun opening
Grandfather and grandmother are here
Feel the cool ground beneath me
Feel their hot whisper in my ear

Spiritual sun lifting
My prayers take form with powerful intention
All my relations surround and hear me
My humble prayers rise in ascension

Spiritual sun vortex
Soul cries with passionate release
My spirit transcends all boundaries
I am touched by infinite peace

Spiritual sun illumination
Energy of spirit shines bright
The way has been lighted
I move forward with confident might

Spiritual sun healing

Through me Eagle medicine flows

Shaman healing shaman wisdom

Many lives transformed I know

Spiritual sun knowing

My consciousness expands

Brother Lynx the knower of all secrets

The promise for all life commands

For now Spiritual Sun has awakened

Within me it grows strong

Into the future I travel

I take my place where I belong

Aho mitakuye oyasin!!

Eternal Maternal

Another trip around the Sun
Brings wonderful Mother's Day
The one who cares for all
And starts us on our way

Mother and child a nurturing union
Blessed is the connection
Mother's inviting womb and breast
Through all loving affection

Mother's heart overflowing with love
The ultimate goddess's expression
Forever united together as one
Spirit and grace, unity in perfection

Mother's encouragement through all life's struggles
Her knowing reaps ever expanding good
Picking ourselves up and trying again
Our knowing that we could

For a Mother's heart is continually giving

Loving and expansive in its measure

We are thankful and eternally grateful

For a Mother is truly a treasure!

Sacred Fire, Ancient Wisdom

Sacred fire opens blessed door
Receiving all my relations
Holy smoke fills all directions
Deepening manifestations

Beating water drum calls my soul
Chanting prayers rise to Father sky
Ah Puch, feared God of Xibalba
Stares back with ominous skull eyes

Fiery black coals reveal truth
Skulls of the ancients from all time
Wisdom of the ages is imbued
Understanding enters sublime

Thousands of souls in the darkness
Purple fiery flame burns within
Reaching out they beckon the light
Achieving balance yang to yin

Hazy smoke unveils a temple

Mayan secrets in jungle vines

Gray stones of knowledge climb above

In still repose the way reclines

Journey through the night breaks new day

Powerful medicine spoken

Eagle takes flight to crescent moon

All that IS within, awoken

Morning of Grace

Morning fog blankets the rising sun
Announcing the gift of a new day
Forever present the Source of One
Seeing the great Joy that guides our way

Soft flowing waves on an endless sea
Reach out to the ever distant shore
Bringing Peace and fulfillment of Life
To the here now and forever more

Cardinal sounds a glorious note
Lifting the inner presence within
Feeling Love and bliss from the Divine
Angels in sweet unison chime in

Dew drops glisten in the morning sun
Embracing spiritual light of now
As awakening grass grows by itself
Knowing transformation shows the how

Whispering wind rustles the tree leaves
Speaking Truth that resides in all things
Immersed in the presence of thy Grace
And the wondrous gratitude it brings

Water birthing a beautiful lotus
Rose colored petals kissing the sky
Reflections from the eternal Source
Reveals delicate nuances of why

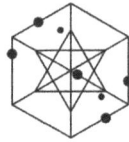

Divine Summation

Peaceful heart giving of itself
Imbues light from a spiritual sun
Gentle guiding force shows the path
To the truest right way of One

Deeper beauty stirs from within
Filling the Soul with wondrous love
Immersed Being with all that IS
Transcends to a place far above

Faith lifts thy spirit upon high
Heaven's kiss of inspiration
Energy flowing through all things
The presence of great summation

Universe ever expanding
One true Power behind it all
Consciousness always evolving
Spirit's discernment heeds the call

Energy of thought manifests
Into all forms of thy desire
Feeling and belief transforms All
Truth and dreams set to conspire

Gratitude in full engagement
Blessed joy felt in elation
Life's secrets revealed in knowing
God's Grace in Divine creation

Journey to Oneness

Warm, gentle breezes brush palm leaves
Announcement of the setting sun
Apprehensive breathing fills me
Journey preparation to One

Final sacred breath takes my soul
Setting sun on a dying world
Mystic explosion reigns within
To abysmal depths I am hurled

Vibrating rainbow sea of chaos
One beckons with guttural call
The finite self lost for all time
Blackness consumes immortal hall

Release of what no longer serves
Bright light guides the infinite way
Renewing first breath of one life
Rebirths a glorious new day

Spirit animal takes the lead
The roar of nature's energy
Unchecked infinite power
Ensures eternal synergy

Angels and guides in unity
One truth revealed in how I see
Blessed experiential journey
Blissful peace, pure love are now me

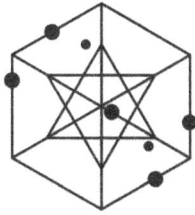

Acknowledgements

This book is more than a collection of poems —
it is a testament to the sacred unfolding of my spiritual
journey...
and to the many souls who have illuminated my path with grace.

To the countless spiritual teachers, mentors, and mystics — seen
and unseen —
whose words, presence, and energy guided me inward:
thank you for helping me remember who I truly am.

Your wisdom awakened deeper currents of divine connection
within me,
and every page of this book carries your imprint.

To the spiritual teachings, sacred texts, and practices that have
shaped my being —from the Tao to tantra, stillness to
surrender, devotion to embodiment —
you have not only expanded my awareness but given me the
language to translate Spirit into form. I bow in reverence.

To my beloved wife, Cristy — thank you for being the soul I
knew before I remembered. Your love, patience, and presence
have been the steady flame beside mine. In every silence, every
poem, every longing — you were there.

You are a living reminder of the divine companioning that love makes possible.

And to all who have walked beside me on this path — in friendship, in spirit, in resonance — thank you.

This offering is ours. These words are not mine alone, but echoes of all we've shared, learned, surrendered, and become.

May these pages serve as a mirror, a balm, and a blessing.

With deepest love and eternal gratitude,
Dr. Bill

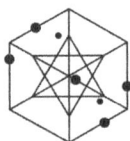

About The Author

Dr. Bill Clark is a modern-day Renaissance man on a mission to help others live beyond limits.

A PhD chemist, spiritual seeker, artist, writer, speaker, and entrepreneur, Dr. Bill bridges the worlds of science and soul through everything he creates. He is the founder of NutriSelect.ai, an AI-powered health tech company revolutionizing personalized supplementation for optimal well-being.

Dr. Bill is also the creator and host of the Beyond Limits Podcast – Where Spirit Meets Science, a weekly series that explores human potential through elevated conversations, spiritual insight, and transformative storytelling. His TEDx talk, *"The 5 Keys to Unlocking Your Spiritual Awakening,"* invites audiences to remember their divine blueprint and embody awakening in real, grounded, and powerful ways.

But his journey began long before the labs and stages.

From climbing trees barefoot as a curious child… to living in a tent with only $11 to his name… to enduring heartbreak, reinvention, and the long walk toward healing, Dr. Bill's life is a testament to resilience, grace, and spiritual awakening.

He is known for guiding others into full-spectrum transformation—physically, emotionally, and energetically—through practical wisdom, poetic insight, and embodied truth.

Dr. Bill lives in Puerto Vallarta, Mexico with the true love of his life, Cristy, their teenage daughter Karla, and their two beloved animal companions: Luna, a spirited Maltese, and Mazikeeno, their mystical Siberian cat.

Whether through books, podcasting, speaking, or soulful innovation, Dr. Bill invites us to align our health, passion, and purpose—so we can live a life that is expansive, inspired, and uniquely our own.

Connect with Dr. Bill

Dr. Bill Clark - www.drbillclark.life

LinkedIn - www.linkedin.com/in/drbillclark/

Instagram - https://www.instagram.com/drbillclark

Facebook - https://www.facebook.com/drbillclark.life/

X (Twitter) - https://x.com/drbillclark

YouTube - https://www.youtube.com/@drbillclark

Other Works by the Author -

"Coming Soon: *The 5 Keys to Unlocking Your Spiritual Awakening* (2025)"

www.ingramcontent.com/pod-product-compliance
Lightning Source LLC
LaVergne TN
LVHW041234080426

835508LV00011B/1207